THIS BOOK BELONGS TO:

_____

Name

_____

Date

_____

_____

_____

TAN · BOOKS

SON OF GOD

THE LIFE OF JESUS CHRIST IN PICTURES

FOREWORD BY ROMA DOWNEY

CONTENTS

FOREWORD

MY HUSBAND MARK BURNETT and I have been working together for five years to bring to the screen the stories of the Bible. It was a blessing that *The Bible* series was watched by 100 million people in the US alone and millions more around the globe. It has been a labor of love for us to breathe fresh visual life into sacred scripture and tell the remarkable story of God and all of us.

While we were shooting the gospels and the life of Jesus we knew the footage was extraordinary and needed to be seen, not just on television but on the big screen.

The story of Jesus is the most important love story that can be told. For God so loved the world that he sent Jesus to bring us home. Jesus who is truly God and truly man. He walked among us. He lived on this earth like the rest of us. He had friends and family. He had joys and sorrows. He chose to become a man and live among us.

We wanted to make *SON OF GOD* so that we can see from his humble birth through his passion, death and resurrection, his extraordinary love and sacrifice for us. We can experience his love and be reminded that we are redeemed from sin and welcomed into eternal life.

As in *The Bible* series I was privileged to play Mary, the Mother of Jesus in *SON OF GOD*.

I was born and raised Catholic in Ireland and have loved the Blessed Mother and her son Jesus my whole life. It was a great honor to portray her on the screen and was one of the most moving experiences of my life. For Mary was not only the Mother of the Son of God but also the mother of a son and those scenes filmed at the foot of the cross were profoundly moving.

It is my hope that through our film *SON OF GOD*, and through this beautiful inspirational book, *Son of God: The Life of Jesus Christ in Pictures* which combines photos from the film with a history of Jesus and his mission, you will be inspired to grow closer to Mary's beloved son as well. May God bless you.

Sincerely,
Roma Downey

JESUS

In the beginning was the Word, and the Word was with God, and the Word was God. He was in the beginning with God; all things were made through him, and without him was not anything made that was made. In him was life, and the life was the light of men. The light shines in the darkness, and the darkness has not overcome it.

—John 1:1–5

JESUS IS THE WORD, the Second Person of the Holy Trinity, the Son of God. He is truly God. And he is truly man.

For a brief span of time God himself, in the person of Jesus Christ, walked among us, ate with us, laughed and cried with us. God became one of us, and ultimately died for us. He gave his life for our sins and on the third day rose again, so that we might rise again from the death of sin and live with him forever.

What follows is the story of Christ's life, when the Son of God walked the earth performing miracles, instituting the sacraments— through which he still lives with us today— establishing his Church, and preaching and teaching the Good News of the Father.

The Good News is a message of love: "For God so loved the world that he gave his only Son, that whoever believes in him should not perish but have eternal life." It is a love that conquers all, even sin and death.

The story of the Son of God is above all else the account of his glorious triumph over suffering and death. Christ's message is timeless. It applies to the whole human race now, as it did when he lived and suffered here on earth, and as it will until the end of time.

MARY

"My soul magnifies the Lord,
And my spirit rejoices in God my
Savior,
For he has regarded the low estate of
his handmaiden.
For behold, henceforth all
generations will call me
blessed."

—Luke 1:46–48

THE STORY OF THE Son of God begins with a woman, for Jesus was truly man as well as God. The Virgin Mary was chosen from all time to have the greatest privilege a creature could enjoy. At God's appointed time, the angel Gabriel entered her home and greeted her: "Hail, full of grace, the Lord is with you!"

The humble girl was troubled by these words. But the angel gently calmed her fears, before breaking the news. "Behold, you will conceive in your womb and bear a son, and you shall call his name Jesus." To Mary, familiar with the prophecies of the Savior, this could mean only one thing: she was to become the mother of Christ.

Mary, as his mother, lived with intimate closeness to Jesus. She shared in his joys, and she also shared in his sorrows, suffering along with him as she watched her beloved son and God endure torture and execution.

Before he died, Jesus entrusted his mother to John, and so to us also. Mary is our mother, too, and she will show us how to love her son as she loved him: with purity and tenderness and with our whole heart.

PETER

Jesus looked at him, and said, "So you are Simon the son of John? You shall be called Cephas" (which means Peter).

—John 1:42

AT THE BEGINNING OF his public ministry, Christ renames Simon, Cephas (or Peter), meaning "Rock." And so it is foretold that Christ will establish his Church upon Peter's leadership.

Peter, a fisherman, is drawn to Jesus right away and takes up Christ's offer to become a "fisher of men." Peter will later be the first of the Apostles to identify Jesus as what he truly is: the Son of God.

Peter often drew rebukes from Jesus for vowing to prevent Christ from suffering. Though he did not fully understand, before the Resurrection, why Jesus must suffer and die, Peter remained fiercely faithful to the Lord.

Peter attempted to defend Jesus in Gethsemane when Jesus was taken to the high priests. Jesus was arrested and Peter drew his sword and claimed he would never leave Jesus' side. Of course, Peter was weak, and later denied Christ three times before the night was over. Yet, Christ sees Peter's sorrow and forgives him.

After Jesus' death and resurrection, Peter became the bishop of Rome and the first pope, steadfastly proclaiming the Good News of Christ with his characteristic passion and love. In the end, he did stay with Christ unto death, eventually being martyred for Christ by crucifixion.

JOHN

One of his disciples, whom Jesus loved, was lying close to the breast of Jesus.

—John 13:23

JOHN WAS THE APOSTLE especially beloved by Christ. He was there for all the great miracles, was present at the Transfiguration, accompanied Jesus to Gethsemane on the night he was betrayed, and was the only Apostle who stayed with Christ through the Crucifixion.

It was John who sat close to Jesus at the Last Supper, laying his head on his Master's chest.

Christ so loved John that, before his death, he entrusted Mary to John as his own mother, and entrusted John to Mary as her son.

After Christ's Ascension, John proclaimed the Good News and established the Church in Asia Minor. He wrote one of the Gospels and three Epistles. He was eventually sentenced to exile on the island of Patmos, where he received a vision from God, which he recounted in the book of Revelation.

John was the lone Apostle who was not martyred, but he endured a sort of martyrdom of his own. He lived in exile until his death, alone, while his brother Apostles all went on to rejoin Jesus in eternity.

JUDAS

So when he had dipped the morsel, he gave it to Judas, the son of Simon Iscariot. Then after the morsel, Satan entered into him.

—John 13:26–27

NOT MUCH IS KNOWN from Scripture about Judas except that he betrayed Jesus and managed the Apostles' money. He was also, according to the Gospel of John, a thief.

Judas knew that the chief priests wished to put an end to Christ's ministry, and so he approached them on his own accord, accepting thirty pieces of silver to betray Jesus. On Holy Thursday, after the Last Supper, Judas carried out his betrayal, indicating to the temple guard who Christ was by kissing him.

While Judas' motivations for betraying Christ are not known, both Luke and John attribute his actions, in part, to being influenced by the devil.

Judas serves as a reminder that even those who are close to Christ can be tempted into sin. We must always remain steadfast, with eyes affixed to Jesus, lest we be drawn away from him.

MARY MAGDALENE

The twelve were with him and also . . . Mary, called Magdalene, from whom seven demons had gone out, and Joanna, the wife of Chuza, Herod's steward, and Susanna, and many others, who provided for them out their means.
—Luke 8:1–3

MARY MAGDALENE, FROM WHOM Jesus cast out seven demons, was a close friend and follower of Christ. She is commonly held to have been the sister of Martha and Lazarus. Mary is one of several important women in the Gospels. She was there at the foot of the cross and she was there when Jesus was placed in the tomb. According to Mark's Gospel, Mary Magdalene was also the first person Jesus appeared to after his Resurrection.

Following Christ's Ascension, tradition holds that this great woman, along with Lazarus and others, converted the area of Marseilles, which today is part of Southern France.

19

PHARISEES

Woe to you, scribes and Pharisees, hypocrites! for you are like whitewashed tombs, which outwardly appear beautiful, but within they are full of dead men's bones and all uncleanness.

—Matthew 23:27

IN THE TIME OF the Maccabees, the Pharisees were a group of Jews who were so devout in observing the laws of God that they often were martyred for their faith. Their faithfulness led them to be esteemed in the Jewish community, but by Jesus' time they clung to the letter of the law, ignoring its spirit. They stood on ceremony and outward appearances, but neglected the deeper laws of love, justice, and mercy.

When Jesus fulfilled the old law with the new commandment to love God above all, and your neighbor as yourself, the Pharisees were threatened, accused him of blasphemy, and constantly tried to trick him into going against the law. The Pharisees alerted Caiaphas and the other chief priests to Jesus' ministry and urged his arrest.

MATTHEW

As Jesus passed on from there, he saw a man called Matthew sitting at the tax office; and he said to him, "Follow me." And he rose and followed him.

—Matthew 9:9

MATTHEW WAS A TAX collector, a profession which, in the time of Jesus, was marked by dishonesty, injustice, and theft. Jesus called Matthew just after healing the paralyzed man not only from his physical infirmity, but from his sins as well.

Matthew was moved that Christ would call him, a sinner, to follow him. In a beautiful moment of faith, Matthew rises from his table—leaving his wealth and worldly possessions behind him—and follows Christ.

Matthew authored the Gospel of Matthew, and, like the other Apostles, went out to spread Jesus' teaching before being martyred for his faith.

THOMAS

Thomas, called the Twin, said to his fellow disciples, "Let us also go, that we may die with him."

—John 11:16

THOMAS SPOKE THESE WORDS after Jesus decided to go to Bethany to raise Lazarus from the dead. The people there had wanted to stone him, and so Jesus was ostensibly risking death. Thomas' words show his great love for Jesus and his faith; a faith that would later be tested, resulting in his famous moniker: Doubting Thomas.

And yet, although Thomas doubted that Christ had appeared to his fellow Apostles in the upper room after his Resurrection, he recovers with a profound statement: "My Lord, and my God."

Thomas went on to the preach the Gospel as far east as India, and there suffered martyrdom, finally fulfilling those words he had spoken before embarking for Bethany: "Let us also go so that we may die with him."

PILATE

So Pilate, wishing to satisfy the crowd, released for them Barabbas; and having scourged Jesus, he delivered him to be crucified.

—Mark 15:15

DURING THE TIME OF Pilate's reign as procurator over Jerusalem, the Jewish people had become increasingly frustrated with Roman rule. Pilate feared that a rebellion could take place at any moment, and thus was a harsh and merciless ruler, often resorting to violence in order to keep the Jews submissive. Roman fears of a Jewish rebellion led the Emperor to give Pilate judicial powers over Jerusalem at a time when most procurators merely took care of financial matters.

It was due to Pilate's role as judge that Jesus was brought before him by the chief priests under charges of blasphemy. Pilate found no fault in Christ and sought to dismiss the case, but the chief priests claimed that Jesus and his followers could stage a rebellion. Fearing an uprising, and fearing for his job, Pilate famously washed his hands of the matter, and gave Jesus up to be crucified.

CAIAPHAS

Then the chief priests and the elders of the people gathered in the palace of the high priest, who was called Caiaphas, and took counsel together in order to arrest Jesus by stealth and kill him.

—Matthew 26:3–4

WHILE JESUS WAS MINISTERING publicly, Caiaphas served as the high priest of the temple in Jerusalem. At that time it was a position given by Roman authority. For this reason Caiaphas, like Pilate, feared a Jewish insurrection.

He was threatened not only by Jesus' teachings, but by the following he had built. Caiaphas was in a tough position. In their own homeland, the Jews were forced to be subservient to the power of the Roman Empire. And so Caiaphas, along with the other chief priests brought Jesus in the dead of night and presided over a sham trial that determined Jesus' guilt. He also was responsible for handing Jesus over to Pilate, encouraging Pilate to crucify Jesus in order to avoid a rebellion.

After the crucifixion and the Resurrection, Caiaphas served for several more years as the Roman-appointed high priest.

NICODEMUS

Now there was a man of the Pharisees, named Nico-
demus, a ruler of the Jews. This man came to Jesus by
night and said to him, "Rabbi, we know that you are
a teacher come from God; for no one can do these signs
that you do, unless God is with him."

—John 3:1–2

NICODEMUS WAS A PHARISEE and a member of the Sanhedrin, the Jewish ruling class. Despite these groups' hostility toward Jesus, Nicodemus saw Jesus' goodness and divine authority, and came to believe that he was the Messiah. Nicodemus defended Jesus among the chief priests, calling for a fair trial. Nicodemus also assisted with Jesus' burial, offering a hundred pounds of myrrh and aloe.

When many of Jesus' other followers had fled, Nicodemus stood by him.

EARLY LIFE

NATIVITY

And the angel said to them, "Be not afraid; for behold, I bring you good news of a great joy which will come to all people; for to you is born this day in the city of David a Savior, who is Christ the Lord."

—Luke 2:10–11

THE ROMAN EMPEROR, AUGUSTUS, issued an edict that all his subjects register in their city of origin. Joseph's family came from Bethlehem, so he was obliged to journey there from Nazareth. Mary knew that she would soon give birth, but with complete trust in God, she set out on the arduous journey. Bethlehem was overcrowded, since many visitors had arrived for the registration. Consequently, the only shelter Joseph could find for his wife was a little stable. Here in this lowly shelter, Mary brought forth the King of Kings.

God had arranged that his Son be paid homage, just after his birth, by those very dear to Christ's heart. We shall see that throughout his life, Jesus favored the poor and the humble. As Mary and Joseph, rapt in loving devotion, bent over the Child, an angel announced the great news to a group of shepherds nearby. These tidings were not revealed to the great ones of Israel, the priests, the scholars, the Pharisees, but rather to poor, humble, sincere shepherds.

The surroundings of poverty and discomfort that God chose for the birth of his Son must carry for us all an important message: self-denial. From his first moment on earth he chose a borrowed stable for his birth, as at death he chose a borrowed grave.

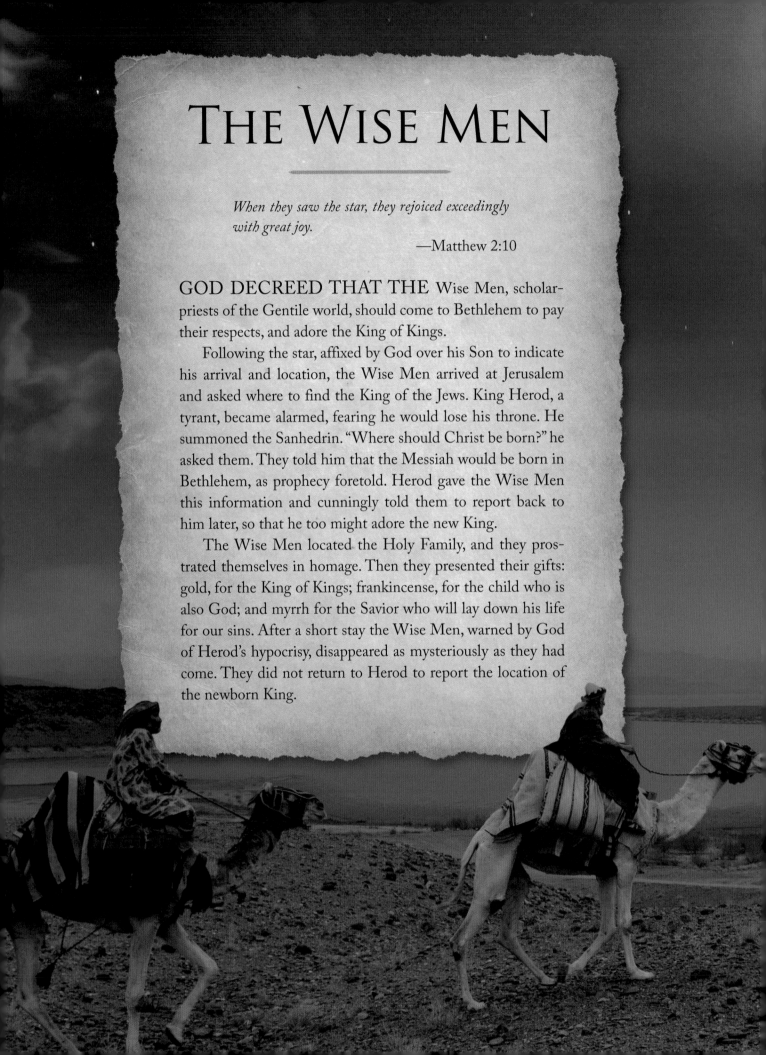

THE WISE MEN

When they saw the star, they rejoiced exceedingly with great joy.

—Matthew 2:10

GOD DECREED THAT THE Wise Men, scholar-priests of the Gentile world, should come to Bethlehem to pay their respects, and adore the King of Kings.

Following the star, affixed by God over his Son to indicate his arrival and location, the Wise Men arrived at Jerusalem and asked where to find the King of the Jews. King Herod, a tyrant, became alarmed, fearing he would lose his throne. He summoned the Sanhedrin. "Where should Christ be born?" he asked them. They told him that the Messiah would be born in Bethlehem, as prophecy foretold. Herod gave the Wise Men this information and cunningly told them to report back to him later, so that he too might adore the new King.

The Wise Men located the Holy Family, and they prostrated themselves in homage. Then they presented their gifts: gold, for the King of Kings; frankincense, for the child who is also God; and myrrh for the Savior who will lay down his life for our sins. After a short stay the Wise Men, warned by God of Herod's hypocrisy, disappeared as mysteriously as they had come. They did not return to Herod to report the location of the newborn King.

FLIGHT INTO EGYPT

This was to fulfill what the Lord had spoken by the prophet, "Out of Egypt have I called my son."
—Matthew 2:15

THOUGH THWARTED FOR THE moment, Herod's cruel designs spelled great danger for the baby Jesus. The night the Wise Men departed, an angel appeared to Joseph in a dream and told him to flee with Christ and Mary into Egypt. Joseph, always obedient, complied instantly. After six or seven days of exhausting travel, they reached Memphis. Here, tradition tells us, they settled for the duration of their stay in Egypt.

Meanwhile, Herod formed an unspeakable plan. Sending for the soldiers of his guard, he ordered them to massacre all male children two years old and under in Bethlehem and its surrounding area. The cruel command was swiftly carried out, and the children shed their blood in martyrdom for the cause of Christ.

A short time after his hideous crime, Herod, tormented by disease, died in agony. Herod thus removed, the angel reappeared to Joseph, and directed him to take the child and his mother back to Israel. So the Holy Family returned from exile and settled in Nazareth.

BAPTISM

"This is my beloved Son, with whom I am well pleased."

—Matthew 3:17

NEWS OF THE MINISTRY of John the Baptist—Jesus' cousin and a hermit who heralded the coming of Christ—had reached Galilee, and a group set out along the Jordan to hear him. One member of this group was Jesus, known to his townsmen as a carpenter. At the Jordan he, with the others, stopped to listen. With these others, unassuming as ever, he stepped forward to be baptized, last of the group. John the Baptist did not at first know who he was, so perfect was Jesus' humility. Yet, even before God revealed it to him, John the Baptist knew that this man should be the one baptizing. This was the one for whom he was herald. Jesus, however, meek and humble, overcame his protests and insisted on being baptized.

Christ's baptism ended his private life, and also foreshadowed the Christian sacrament of Baptism, by which we too become children of God. The words of the Father from heaven after Christ's Baptism—"This is my beloved Son in whom I am well pleased"—are said to us when we die to sin and are brought to new life as a child of God in Baptism.

PUBLIC MINISTRY

FISHERS OF MEN

And Jesus said to Simon, "Do not be afraid; henceforth you will be catching men."

—Luke 5:10

WHEN JESUS CALLED HIS closest disciples—the Apostles—at the outset of his ministry, Peter was among the first. His given name was Simon, and he was a fisherman. One day, Jesus climbed into Simon's boat to preach to the crowd on the shore. Afterwards, he told Simon to cast his nets into the deep. Simon protested, saying that he had been fishing all night, but had caught nothing. Still, Simon had been listening to Jesus' teaching, and so he obeyed.

After casting the nets, at Jesus' behest, Simon pulled in enough fish to fill his boat and his partner's boat. Astonished, Simon asked Jesus to depart from him, a sinful man. But Jesus instead called him to leave his boat and become a fisher of men.

Jesus would give Simon a new name, Peter, which means rock. And this rugged fisherman of great passion and faith would become the first pope: the rock on which Jesus established his Church.

SERMON ON THE MOUNT

IN THIS GREAT SERMON, Jesus proclaimed the Golden Rule—love God above all and your neighbor as yourself. During the Sermon on the Mount Jesus also taught the Beatitudes, which exalt the poor, the meek, and the humble as God's favored ones:

"Blessed are the poor in spirit, for theirs is the kingdom of heaven.

"Blessed are those who mourn, for they shall be comforted.

"Blessed are the meek, for they shall inherit the earth.

"Blessed are those who hunger and thirst for righteousness, for they shall be satisfied.

"Blessed are the merciful, for they shall obtain mercy.

"Blessed are the pure in heart, for they shall see God.

"Blessed are the peacemakers, for they shall be called sons of God.

"Blessed are those who are persecuted for righteousness' sake, for theirs is the kingdom of heaven.

"Blessed are you when men revile you and persecute you and utter all kinds of evil against you falsely on my account.

"Rejoice and be glad, for your reward is great in heaven, for so men persecuted the prophets who were before you."

—Matthew 5:3–12

Jesus Heals the Paralytic

"Man, your sins are forgiven you."

—Luke 5:20

JESUS WAS SPEAKING TO a crowd of people, when some men tried to bring their paralyzed friend to him. The crowd was large, however, and they could not reach Jesus. So they removed the roof from the building and lowered their friend down to Jesus, who, seeing their faith said: "Man, your sins are forgiven."

At once the Pharisees were shocked at this seeming blasphemy and questioned Jesus. So, Jesus asked them:

> *"Why do you question in your hearts? Which is easier, to say, 'Your sins are forgiven you,' or to say, 'Rise and walk'? But that you may know that the Son of man has authority on earth to forgive sins"—he said to the man who was paralyzed— "I say to you, rise, take up your bed and go home." And immediately he rose before them, and took up that on which he lay, and went home, glorifying God.*

—Luke 5:22–25

This miracle is a reminder that for all of Jesus' breathtaking physical miracles, the most important miracle is that Jesus came to wash us clean from sin.

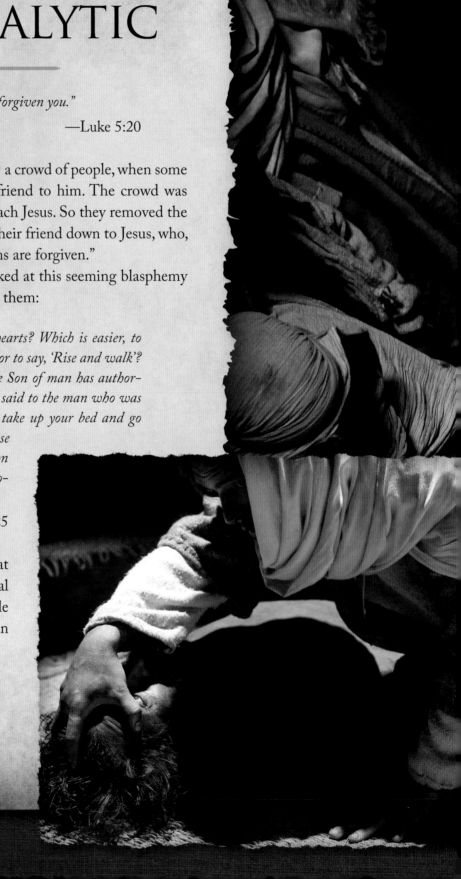

Jesus Forgives the Adulteress

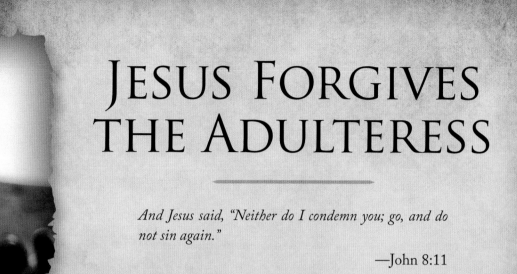

And Jesus said, "Neither do I condemn you; go, and do not sin again."

—John 8:11

THE PHARISEES AND CHRIST'S other enemies, increasingly worried about the following he was gaining, used every opportunity to trap Jesus into going against Jewish law. One day, they brought to him a woman accused of adultery. Citing the law of Moses they asked what her sentence should be. He told them, "Let him who is without sin among you be the first to throw a stone at her." The Pharisees and others in the crowd who had picked up stones in order to carry out their sentence stood still. Then, they dropped their stones and slunk away one by one, for, of course, none of them could say that they were without sin.

Jesus asked the woman where the Pharisees had gone, and asked if anyone had cast a stone. She answered that no one had condemned her. Jesus replied, "Neither do I condemn you; go, and do not sin again."

Here Jesus shows that God alone can judge. And yet Jesus, who is God, shows mercy upon the sinner. But he also exhorts the sinner to renounce sin. While Jesus forgives us for our sins, he also requires us to be truly repentant and to fight against sin.

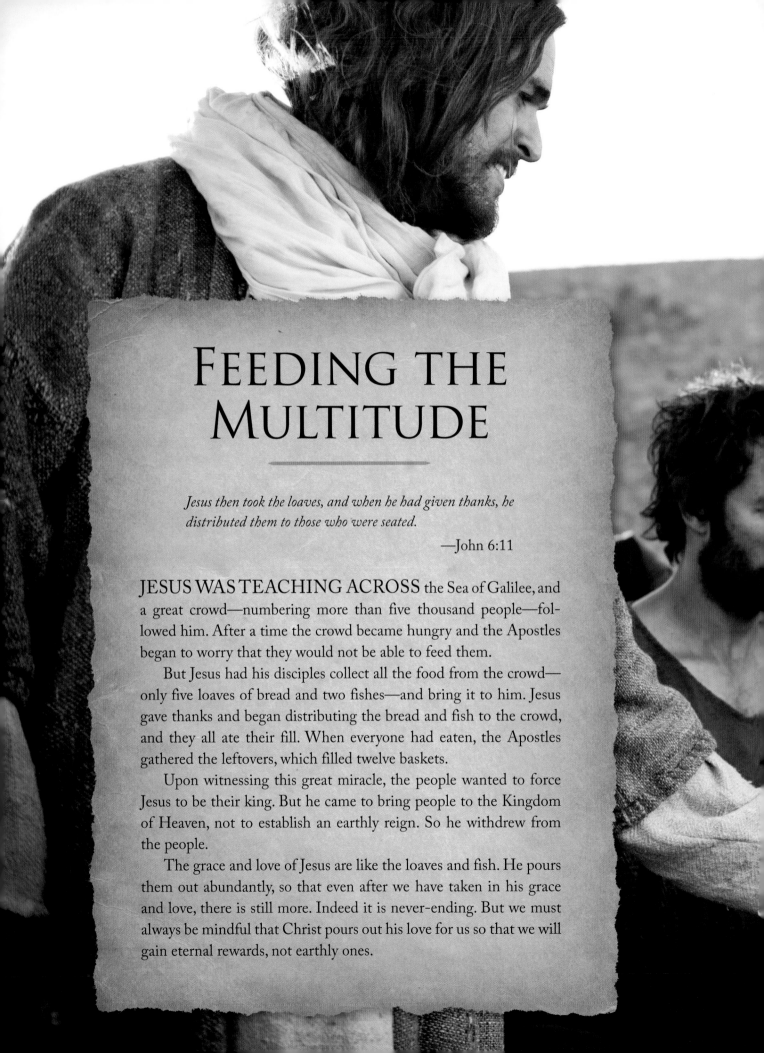

FEEDING THE MULTITUDE

*Jesus then took the loaves, and when he had given thanks, he
distributed them to those who were seated.*

—John 6:11

JESUS WAS TEACHING ACROSS the Sea of Galilee, and
a great crowd—numbering more than five thousand people—followed him. After a time the crowd became hungry and the Apostles
began to worry that they would not be able to feed them.

But Jesus had his disciples collect all the food from the crowd—
only five loaves of bread and two fishes—and bring it to him. Jesus
gave thanks and began distributing the bread and fish to the crowd,
and they all ate their fill. When everyone had eaten, the Apostles
gathered the leftovers, which filled twelve baskets.

Upon witnessing this great miracle, the people wanted to force
Jesus to be their king. But he came to bring people to the Kingdom
of Heaven, not to establish an earthly reign. So he withdrew from
the people.

The grace and love of Jesus are like the loaves and fish. He pours
them out abundantly, so that even after we have taken in his grace
and love, there is still more. Indeed it is never-ending. But we must
always be mindful that Christ pours out his love for us so that we will
gain eternal rewards, not earthly ones.

RAISING OF LAZARUS

LAZARUS, A GOOD FRIEND of Jesus, had become seriously ill and was near death. Jesus heard the news from Lazarus' sisters, Martha and Mary, but did not go to meet them.

But after a few days, Jesus suddenly told the disciples to get ready to go to Bethany, for Lazarus, their friend, was dead.

As Jesus and the Twelve approached the house, Martha came running to meet them. Coming up to Jesus she told him that Lazarus would not have died had Jesus been there; but that if he asked God, Lazarus would be raised. Here we see that faith and trust that Jesus always rewards. Then Mary, frantic in her love, ran to him and threw herself at his feet, pouring out her grief. Profoundly touched, Christ wept.

They made their way to the tomb and Jesus began to pray to God. Then in a loud voice he said, "Lazarus, come forth." It was an awesome moment. Lazarus came walking out of the tomb, bound in his death shroud.

The raising of Lazarus was accomplished to sow faith in the hearts of men. Jesus did not, while on earth, remove pain and death, but rather he taught that suffering can lead us to God, if accepted in the right spirit. Even death, the climax of suffering, is not the end, but the beginning of a new life in his Kingdom.

Jesus Fulfills Scripture

AFTER BEING TEMPTED BY Satan in the desert, Jesus returned home to Nazareth. On the Sabbath, he went to the synagogue and began to read from the book of Isaiah. He read:

> *"The Spirit of the Lord is upon me,*
> *because he has anointed me to*
>   *preach good news to the poor.*
> *He has sent me to proclaim release*
>   *to the captives*
> *and recovering of sight to the blind,*
> *to set at liberty those who are oppressed,*
>   *to proclaim the acceptable year of the Lord."*
>
> —Luke 4:18–19

Jesus then told those who were listening: "Today this scripture has been fulfilled in your hearing." But the people doubted, saying, "Are you not Joseph's son?" And Jesus told them that no prophets are welcome in their homeland, and that he would not heal or perform miracles in Nazareth. The people sought to kill him, but he passed right among them, unharmed.

HOLY WEEK

THE LAST SUPPER

"This is my body, which is given for you."

—Luke 22:19

EARLY THURSDAY MORNING, THE day of the Pasch, Jesus sent Peter and John to Jerusalem to find a room and prepare for the paschal meal. That evening, Jesus and the rest of the Apostles joined them there. Before supper, Christ set an example of humility by washing their feet.

Jesus then blessed and broke bread and giving it to them bade them eat it saying, "This is my body." Then he took the cup and giving thanks gave it to them with the words, "This cup which is poured out for you is the new covenant in my blood." With these words Jesus linked forever the ceremony of the Last Supper with his glorious Sacrifice on Calvary, and so instituted the sacrament of the Eucharist, through which Christ offers us his body and blood at every Mass.

At this time, Jesus also instituted the priesthood, giving the Apostles the power to offer the sacrifice of the Eucharist, using his words.

AGONY IN THE GARDEN

"My Father, if it be possible, let this cup pass from me; nevertheless, not as I will, but as thou wilt."

—Matthew 26:39

AFTER SUPPER, JESUS SET out for the Mount of Olives. Coming to the garden of Gethsemane, Jesus led the Apostles to an olive grove. Jesus took Peter, James, and John with him apart from the others. He wanted their comforting presence, but withdrew to pray alone. Horrified in his human nature at the vision of his coming sufferings, his heart was filled with sorrow for the sins of man, and he cried out: "My Father, if it be possible, let this cup pass from me; nevertheless, not as I will, but as thou wilt." This is the model for us in all suffering. There is no misery or vexation that will not be relieved in a heart that can still murmur, "Thy will be done."

During this phase of suffering, an angel appeared and strengthened him. Yet even with this help, Jesus' agony was so intense that blood oozed forth from the pores of his body. Returning to Peter, James, and John to seek solace, he found them asleep. He chided them, and went back to his prayer and agony. Later, he returned, and again found them asleep. Without a word he went back to face the third and last phase of his agony: his betrayal.

JESUS BEFORE THE HIGH PRIEST

And they all said, "Are you the Son of God then?" And he said to them, "You say that I am."

—Luke 22:70

AFTER JESUS' AGONY, JUDAS led members of the Sanhedrin, accompanied by temple guards and Roman soldiers, to arrest Christ. Jesus, accepting God's plan for him, went willingly. He healed the ear of one of his captors—Malchus—after Peter cut it off in an attempt to save Jesus.

Christ was brought to Caiaphas' palace where witnesses testified falsely that he had blasphemed. Jesus, calm and dignified throughout this mockery of justice, announced categorically that he was the Savior, and truly the Son of God. That was all Caiaphas needed. The chief priests voted for his execution, and sent Jesus to Pilate to ratify the sentence.

Consider the uncomplaining Christ who bore all this agony voluntarily to atone for our sins. Through our suffering runs self-concern; through his shines love.

PETER'S DENIAL

Peter again denied it; and at once the cock crowed.

—John 18:27

AFTER JESUS' ARREST, THE Apostles fled, as Christ had told them they would just hours before. Peter had protested, saying that he would never leave Jesus' side. Christ replied that even before the cock crowed the next morning, Peter would deny him three times.

Peter, ashamed of his fear, soon returned and followed a short distance behind Christ's captors. But soon, his resolve was again shaken. Inside the palace Peter was asked if he were not one of Christ's disciples. He replied, "I am not." Then he joined other servants warming themselves around a fire in the courtyard, where a maid-servant told him that he looked like one of the Twelve. Indignantly, he denied it. Still standing by the fire, Peter was asked once again if he was one of the Twelve. This time he denied that he even knew Jesus. An hour later some servants told him they were sure he was a follower of Jesus. Peter swore vehemently that he did not know Christ. During these denials the unmistakable crowing of a cock was heard three times. Later, as Jesus was led from the palace, he fixed on Peter a searching look. His heart crushed, Peter fled from the palace in distraction, and burst into bitter tears. And yet Jesus forgave Peter.

In the bitter tears of our own periods of desolation, let us avail ourselves of Jesus' sympathy, love, and forgiveness, which he is ever ready to extend to all who ask.

THE SCOURGING

AFTER THE SHAM TRIAL before the high priest, Jesus was sent to Pilate, who was impressed by the dignified bearing of Christ. So he returned Jesus to the Sanhedrin, and said he saw no reason for their accusations. But the chief priests and other leaders intimated that releasing Jesus could stir up a rebellion.

Pilate, in his weakness, had Jesus scourged and beaten. It was the beginning of the great physical punishment Jesus would undergo in order to save us from our sins.

PILATE SENTENCES JESUS

AFTER THE SCOURGING, SOME soldiers fashioned a crown of thorns and shoved it on Jesus' head. It was their mock coronation of "the King of the Jews."

Pilate then presented a battered Jesus before the people, picked by the chief priests to ensure Christ's death. They clamored for Jesus to be crucified. Pilate then gave them a choice between two prisoners to be released to them: Barabbas, a criminal and rebel, or Jesus. The people shouted for Barabbas. Finally, Pilate, fearing a rebellion and the loss of his position, gave in.

He washed his hands of the matter, acquiescing to the demands of the crowd. Jesus would be crucified on Calvary.

The Carrying of the Cross

JESUS, ALONG WITH TWO criminals, was forced to carry his cross to Calvary, the place of the skull, a hill just outside the city walls. Already scourged, beaten, and crowned with thorns, it took all his strength to drag the cross to his place of execution.

But Christ persevered, carrying not only the heavy cross, but the weight of all of our sins on his shoulders. In a tremendous act of love Jesus stumbled through the streets, falling three times, enduring the jeers and mockery of the crowd and the beatings of the soldiers.

It is an act of love that we can never hope to repay. And yet the ultimate sacrifice is still to come.

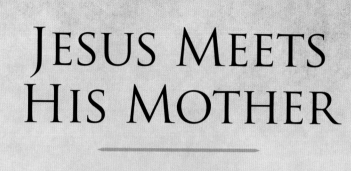

Jesus Meets His Mother

ALONG THE WAY TO Calvary, some of Jesus' followers dotted the crowd, trying to get one last glimpse of their Master. Our Lady was among them, and at one point managed to break through the crowd and approach her beloved son.

Simeon had foretold at the presentation in the temple that Mary would share in the great sorrow and suffering of her son, and in this meeting those words began to be fulfilled. Mary, the Mother of God, who herself lived a life free from sin, watched helplessly as her son endures horrible pain and abject humiliation for us sinners.

She, who bore him and raised him, who tended to him as child, who comforted him, is now powerless to help. But they come together briefly on the road to Calvary, and Mary is able to bring some bit of joy, however small and fleeting, to her son amidst his great suffering.

Mary is our Mother, too, and if we go to her she will offer us comfort, just as she comforted her son.

Simon Helps Jesus Carry the Cross

ALONG THE WAY, THE soldiers realize that Jesus will not make it to Calvary. He has already endured so much physical pain, and is utterly exhausted. So they pull a man from the crowd to help him: Simon of Cyrene.

Simon was a visitor to Jerusalem and not a follower of Jesus. But he gives some relief to the suffering Jesus. An involuntary helper, he nonetheless gave aid and sympathy to Jesus when he needed it most.

Tradition holds that Simon's sons, Rufus and Alexander, became missionaries for the Christian faith.

CRUCIFIXION & RESURRECTION

JESUS EMBRACES THE CROSS

And when they came to the place which is called The Skull, there they crucified him, and the criminals, one on the right and one on the left.

—Luke 23:33

JESUS, AT LAST, HAS arrived at Calvary, where he will complete his passion. The soldiers continue to mock him and the people jeer at him. They strip off his clothes, which tears open his wounds once more. Exhausted and beaten, Jesus crawls to his cross.

Christ died for us. And he did so willingly. Indeed, at any moment he could have removed himself, or called down angels to lift him away. And yet Jesus endures the uncharitable crowds and the violent centurions, the injustice of the scheming chief priests and the spineless Pilate. He endures the long, painful march to Calvary.

Finally, on this hill of death, he climbs onto his cross, broken and beaten, so that he can offer up one last supreme gesture of love for us. He will die for us and our sins. Jesus, who is God, will lay down his life for us. We can never repay him, but, like him, we can embrace our crosses and our sufferings. We can offer them up for him and for others out of love.

We can crawl to our own crosses, dying to sin and ourselves, so that we may live for him.

JESUS ON THE CROSS

"Father, forgive them; for they know not what they do."

—Luke 23:34

EVEN AFTER BEING NAILED to the cross, the people and soldiers continued to deride Jesus. Above him they place the inscription, in mockery, "The King of the Jews."

Nearly dead, Jesus utters a few more words, showing once again his divine character. Magnanimous to the last, he shows mercy on his crucifiers, forgiving them for their actions. Perhaps these kind words, even in the midst of his great suffering, helped lead to the conversion of one of the soldiers. Longinus, who tradition holds would later pierce Jesus' side, became a great saint.

One of the thieves who had been crucified with Jesus began to mock him. He sneered that if Jesus truly were the Messiah, surely he would save them all from their execution. The other thief rebuked him, saying Jesus had done nothing wrong, and asking Jesus to remember him in his Kingdom. Jesus responds to this show of faith and contrition: "Truly, I say to you, today you will be with me in Paradise."

Here, in Jesus' words of forgiveness and salvation, we see his divine mission of love lived out until the very last. No sin is so great that Jesus cannot redeem it through his passion, death, and Resurrection, if only we accept his love and atone for our sins.

Jesus Entrusts Mary to John

When Jesus saw his mother, and the disciple whom he loved standing near, he said to his mother, "Woman, behold your son!" Then he said to the disciple, "Behold, your mother!"

—John 19:26–27

EVER A LOVING SON, Jesus turns to his mother. She is there at the foot of the cross, never leaving his side. She has shared in his sorrow, grief, and pain. Jesus makes sure that she is cared for. He commits her to his beloved disciple, John. So, too, he commits her to us. She is our mother. And we are her children.

She never left the side of Jesus, and she never blackened her soul with sin. She will comfort us, like she comforted Jesus. She will show us how to follow him as she followed him. And she will intercede with him on our behalf.

Jesus Dies on the Cross

AT NOON, THE HEAVENS marked their disapproval and cast over the dreadful scene a curtain of gloom, which continued until three o'clock. Shortly before that fatal hour, Jesus' entire human nature rose in final distress, and a cry of utter agony escaped from his lips, "My God, my God, why hast thou forsaken me?" No words could better portray the extremity of Christ's sufferings.

How consoling for us to know that even Jesus, in his human nature, understands the temptation to despair! But his cry is not ultimately a despairing one. It is a quote from Psalm 22, which, centuries before, predicted the Passion—and the Resurrection.

Then Jesus uttered his last words, entrusting himself to the Father by quoting Psalm 31: "Father into thy hands I commend my spirit." Then with a final cry of pain, Our Savior, victim for our sins on the altar of the cross, bowed his head and died, our salvation bought.

RESURRECTION

And behold, there was a great earthquake; for an angel of the Lord descended from heaven and came and rolled back the stone, and sat upon it.

—Matthew 28:2

EARLY ON SUNDAY MORNING, Mary Magdalene and some other women went to the tomb to care for Jesus' body. They hoped to find someone to help them roll back the stone. But when they arrived they found the stone had already been moved and the soldiers were lying terrified on the ground. Afraid and astonished, they were told by an angel that Jesus was not there, but had risen, as he said he would. Mary Magdalene turned and ran to the Apostles. They did not believe her, but Peter and John ran to the tomb. John allowed Peter to enter first, and Peter saw the tomb empty except for the folded burial linens. Then John came in and looked around the empty tomb. In the words of Scripture, "He saw and believed."

Peter and John returned home after seeing the empty tomb, but Mary Magdalene remained. There Jesus appeared to her and told her to go tell the disciples that he had risen. Later that night, they saw him for themselves when he appeared to them in the Upper Room, where they had held the Last Supper two days before.

Jesus appeared to them, saying, "Peace be with you." He showed them the wounds in his hands and his side and they were overjoyed. Then he breathed on them and said: "Receive the Holy Spirit. If you forgive the sins of any, they are forgiven; if you retain the sins of any, they are retained."

Christ's resurrection is the climax and final triumph of his life on earth. His conquest of sin is victory over suffering and death— the legacy of sin. In him and through him we, too, can conquer suffering and death, and turn all life's trials into ultimate triumph.

DOUBTING THOMAS

"Blessed are those who have not seen and yet believe."
—John 20:29

WHEN JESUS APPEARED TO the Apostles in the Upper Room, Thomas was not there. And when they told him, he did not believe, saying: "Unless I see in his hands the print of the nails, and place my finger in the mark of the nails, and place my hand in his side, I will not believe."

Eight days later, all the Apostles were again together. This time Thomas was with them. Though the doors were shut, Jesus again appeared. He approached Thomas, telling him to look at his wounds and place his hand in his side. Jesus then exhorted him not to be "faithless, but believing." Thomas responded, "My Lord, and my God!" Jesus then praised all those throughout history who have not seen and yet believed.

Jesus, the son of Mary, and yet the Son of God, truly is God. He is our Lord and our God.

Through his teaching he fulfilled the old law with a law of love: love for God and love for our neighbor. And through his passion and death he lived out that law of love for us, washing away our sins. Through his Resurrection he has raised us from death to eternal life, if we believe. Without seeing, let us believe and echo those words of Thomas, "My Lord and my God!"

Photography Credit: Joe Alblas and Casey Crafford

For more information on the motion picture SON OF GOD visit: www.ShareSonofGod.com

Cataloging-in-Publication data on file with the Library of Congress

ISBN: 978-1-61890-589-5

Published by
TAN Books
PO Box 410487
Charlotte, NC 28241
www.TANBooks.com

Printed and bound in the United States of America

Publisher	Robert M. Gallagher
VP Publishing	Conor Gallagher
VP New Business	Rick Rotondi
Editors	Paul Thigpen
	Christian Tappe
Marketing Director	Kevin Gallagher
Trade Sales Director	Brian Kennelly
Parish Sales Director	Jason Oakes
Production Director	Bob Wirtel
Art Director	Mara Persic
Graphic Artist	Caroline Kiser
Digital Marketing	Tarina Weese

TAN Books offers special discounts to schools, parishes, businesses and nonprofit organizations for books purchased as gifts, premiums, promotions, or for educational use. Interested parties may contact our special sales department at 1-800-437-5876 or by email at specialsales@tanbooks.com.

Special Thanks to:
Mark Burnett, Roma Downey, Matthew Haas, Brooke Haas, Mishy Turner,
Randy Sollenberger, Paul Lauer, John Kilcullen,

And to:
Fr. John Bradley
Requiem aeternam dona ei, Domine, et lux perpetua luceat ei